I HAVE NO PLACE IN THE KINGDOM

Poems, Verses, and
Whispers in Revolt

By

Bella Rose Prince

I Have No Place In the Kingdom

ISBN: 979-8-9933209-0-8

Editor: Terry Wolverton
Copyeditor: Kristin Gustafson
Designer: Anamaria Stefan
Illustrator: F.W.
Cover Artist: Riverry Studio

First Edition

POETIC OUTLAWS ONLY

Dedicated to my twin sister, Olivia.
When life crushed my heart to bits, your love was always the resin.
You are the antidote to my darkness
and the reason it has never been able to swallow me whole.
You always have one hand pulling me out,
the other holding a flickering lantern of hope.

Contents

Introduction

I Have No Place in the Kingdom

Neither king nor queen. A joker or a worker bee.
Nor knight nor peasant, not a stable boy or a pheasant.
I roam the halls of the castle, not part of the hustle, the hassle.
I am in the royal family yet not a part of its official history.
If this were a fairytale, I'd never be mentioned.
In a mirror, I'd have no reflection.
I'm here but I'm not.
I simply cannot be bought.
Ample room yet no place for me.
The only thing money can't make you is free.
Golden handcuffs, I call their bluff.
They can't pay for my loyalty, can't pray away cruelty.
They might be royal to the masses, but to me, they're assassins.
Of spirit and soul, they hoard them like gold.
I'll never get on my knees and obey;
I'd rather run than sit still and stay.
It's better to be on the outs than the ins—
Being on the outs is where life begins.
Diamonds, rubies, and thrones hold no power over me.
Don't give a damn about this shiny family tree.
I prefer to be free; I prefer to fly.
Their wings clipped, birds deprived of sky.

I have no place in their kingdom.
No place in this system.
To those who do—
I don't envy you.

Monsters, Villains, and Dragons

No Choice

What all little girls don't know
Is that they have no choice
But to grow up
to become soldiers.
That the world will become their battlefield.

Crimson Beast

Once every month, like clockwork,
Women metamorphosize
Into beasts with curling nails,
Fangs dripping with crimson

Our bodies contort, break, reconfigure
Emotions are pulled by the moon
Self-destruction is our number one desire
But, if not the self, then it's everybody else

The world becomes a treacherous forest
Where creatures lurk and glowing eyes blink
Our minds race inside our skulls,
Rats in a maze with no way out

Our bodies drip, ooze, pulse
As we stalk the haunted woods
Hunting our prey,
Yet you'd never know

We smile and giggle and charm,
Yet remain stoic soldiers on the battlefield
We sit still, look pretty, and obey—
We've mastered our facades

We fake it, not till we make it,
But till we can't take it—
We can always take it
We've trained since birth

Underneath pleasantry and civility
Lies a hairy beast
With sharp claws
And a desire for destruction

Gold and Envy

Big bad monster with teeth made of razors
Bottles of vodka, gallons of chasers
Fancy cars, fancy names
Dropping them like we're one and the same

Politician one weekend, a global star the next
Jesus invited you to his penthouse, I bet
She hoards her gold like it's the damn apocalypse
You take a step too close, a trap wire trips

She dangles it like a carrot in your face
Grabbing your hand to run, but she already tied your lace
It's not enough for her to win, I must also fail
Not your ordinary beast, but she has horns and a tail

She reeks of trauma, self-hatred, and shame
They ooze from her snakeskin as she points blame
Monsters like her don't bite, they talk
They don't just watch, they prey on and stalk

Envy is their biggest crime
They'll look at you, copy and mime
Imitation is the highest form of flattery
Even with her treasures, she'd rather be me

Humane Slaughter

Scared, alone, screeching, and crawling
Babies ripped apart from their mothers, bawling
Ripped open, gutted, tossed aside like trash
You want me to spare your feelings, but Imma be fucking brash

Every bite, every lick, every swallow you take
Every casserole, every cake, every dish you bake
Was an innocent, living soul with a desire to breathe
It wasn't your life to take, not your heartbeat to cease

Here you are entitled to your cravings, beholden to your taste buds
As these innocent creatures' heads fall. One by one. Thud . Thud.
Thud.
If I could look into each and every one of their eyes,
I'd promise they were going to be okay, but my words would be lies

Sweet creatures given no choice but to ache and suffer
Words like "hamburger" and "hotdog" just provide a buffer
To relieve humans of the gore and guilt on their hands
To make them feel less murderous as they eat their prey canned

That corpse once had a perspective, a purpose, a desire
No longer with us, just getting crispy in your oven's fire
So, sure, turn a blind eye, blame everything but us
We sure as hell don't deserve any animals' trust

The slice of pie on your plate drips with blood and flesh
Keep chewing in ignorance on your "food" that's so *fresh*

Knife in the Back

Backstabbing bitch
You smile but I see the twitch
Like a rattlesnake's tail
Your envy likes to see me fail

False like a puppet with a master
You think you're quick, but I'm faster
Fake giggles—those should be illegal
You look down at me like you're so regal

Forget heartbreak, this was betrayal
You never cared about me, just your portrayal
You're Apate, the Goddess of deceit
You broke up with me over text, yeah, I got the receipt

You're the farthest thing from a girl's girl
When I see old photos of us, I want to hurl
I trusted you, loved you, bared my soul
Now when you see my picture, you just fucking scroll

You were my sister, my best friend, a part of my heart
When I think of old memories, they're not sweet, just tart
I will never trust a woman again
I thought only men lie, but women pretend

No such thing as best friends, only good ones
No such thing as blinding trust, there is none
You pulled a Julias Cesear after seventeen long years
When your man wanted us gone, you said, "I volunteer"

You're more dangerous than fanged monsters in the night
Because you're a closet villain hidden in plain sight
You should be an actress for your Oscar winning performance
Should have known you weren't like me—you're just a conformist

Fake feminism, fake girlhood, fake everything you ever said
But it's not me who will suffer, it's you who has to sleep in his bed

Citadel Cell

Try Harder

"Please love me," I whispered.
"I'm trying," I whisper back to myself.

Sugar and Salt

Blood splatter
Heart shattered
Broken limbs
Broken bones
What's the matter
Hate served on a silver platter
I'm tryna find a place called home

Give me some sugar
Give me some spice
Pull the loaded trigger
Don't be fucking nice
The world is tough
A rock tumbled rough
Spinning and spinning
I'm not fucking winning
Winner winner chicken dinner
Never an angel, always the sinner

Caught in its web
Caught in its grasp
I'm a nobody
They say "no" when I ask
Dark and wet
Like a crumbled cave

Climbing and climbing
For something I crave
Give me some sugar
Give me some salt
I know I'm this way
But it's not my damn fault

Try living
While you're trying to survive
Try surviving
While you're trying to die
They say the ground is flat,
But why am I falling?
Down to my knees
Just crawling and bawling

I may smile
I may tell you I'm fine
But if you dig deeper,
I've got a tainted bloodline
How to influence people and make friends,
How to fake it all to the very fucking end

Give me some sugar, give me some brine
If I could change it all, I'd sprint back in time
Back to when I was a blank slate
Back to when I believed in innocence and fate
I try my best, but it's never enough
Who would have thought loving life would be so tough?

Daegu Boy

Each flash pokes a hole through my armor
Protection I crafted with every scream and cry
I don't think people realize I'm just like them:
A person with a heart and soul, just tryna survive

You can humiliate me, shame me, call me nasty names,
But I've done worse to myself, way before this fame
I've gone to the trenches and back in this mind maze before,
So please pummel me into the ground—my inner child begs for more

I guess I deserve this life, this hell, this sin,
Why don't we just crap all over this world we're in
You can't destroy the soul of a soulless man
Can't stop a life before it even began

This is nothing compared to how dark my mind can go,
You'll never know the real me—no, thank God, you'll never know
My heart drenched in gasoline, each flash, a lighted match
There's me and then there's him. Good thing I've learned to detach

A bridge's view has never looked so nice
Hell, I'm being forced to roll the dice
Of being human, being flawed—a fallen angel if you will
Went from God to criminal overnight, damn, what a thrill

I never learned to fly with wings
Flight come to those who bloom in spring
But I bloom in fiery pits of despair—
I don't have wings, just a flimsy prayer

Limerence

Addiction. Obsession. Dopamine rush.
Give me something to live for, something to touch.
Every waking thought and every sleeping nightmare
Just more traps, more vessels to ensnare.

Pick your poison. Pick your wine.
I'm bound by the wrists with duct tape and twine.
Scratch twine—make it ribbons, pretty with a bow.
How can something be so beautiful when I'm at my lowest low?

It whispers first. Then screams. Then yells.
Drags me by the hair, it doesn't ask, it tells.
Disguised with smiles and humor and just plain fun,
Until I'm swallowed by its magnitude, with nowhere to run.

Like Jonah in the whale, it's dark and cold.
But I keep coming back to watch my trauma unfold.
It's shiny and enticing like a siren at night,
But when I lean in closer, it moves to bite.

Jonesing for an escape from my maze-like brain,
With no way out, it's just playing games.
So I lean into comfort, familiarity, the known—
My drug of choice, my fantasies of stories untold.

Maladaptive daydreaming, limerence, delusion
Just to escape the world and the fucked-up institutions.
Not all drugs are created equal,
But all drugs remind me: before now, there was a prequel

Full of shame and darkness and a whole lot of bullshit.
Instead of blaming the world, I look inward and nitpick.
That shame grows like a balloon pumped with air,
Then I look to the world begging for someone to care.

That's when it finds me: drugs, delusion, fantasy.
Instead of a soul, I just become damn anatomy.
Let me escape, let me run, let me hide—
Let me heal the little girl who cried.

Corrupted Youth

Tears drip down my face
Salty pools of empty waste
The realization that I am nothing—I can try
But I can't take nothing and make something

I'll never be happy, yeah, that much is true
I'll never be yellow or orange, just blue
Is it childhood trauma or just bad luck?
I try to sprint and climb, but I'm a sitting duck

Salty oceans, salty tears
Corrupted youth and wasted years
How many tears does it take to fill a damn lake?
I smile and smile, but it's so obviously fake

Some people just feel the world so deeply
Some burst with joy, but I'm so damn sleepy
A dark cloud follows my every step
Perhaps it's the demise I haven't yet met

I'm swallowed by the monster under my bed
I can't stop the poison; it's just going to spread
First to my body, then my mind, my soul
Until I'm swallowed into the deepest darkest hole

I'm already there. Hello? Can you hear me?
Are you receiving this message? Who cares, just let me be
Why me? Why this? Why now? Why then?
I'm an adult covered in soot, like I was when I was ten

What is it like to see the sun shine so bright?
Please, I just want one tiny glimpse of the light
I'm falling and falling deeper into the abyss
Don't worry, I'm good at faking it— you won't know anything's amiss

Tap

Tap tap tap tap tap goes the machine
Tell the doc I'm turning blue instead of green
Some days I'm up, others I'm down
Sometimes *why so serious*; others, imma clown

What is the point of this life so dark?
What is the purpose of a nice walk in the park?
They say everywhere I go, there I am
Never the idol, just the anxious fan

Woopity doo da, 'round and 'round we go
You'll never know who your real friends are, no, you'd never know
When I go low, they miraculously go high
Belittle me, I dare you, go ahead and try

You better watch out because I don't cry—I bite
Thick skin is what you build in darkness not light
Trying to become softer like a dove in the night
But turning a hawk into a jay is less fun and more fight

To-do lists running after me like it will save the day
All these shitty feelings I strain to keep at bay
Some children born into soft, loving arms
Others born just to be slaughtered at farms

Tap tap tap goes the machine in my brain
Don't try to compete with me; stay in your damn lane
Darkness exists so that light can shine
One day, I hope I can call this life mine

Superstar

I got one hand in hell and the other on my guitar.
I'm on a treadmill running, but I can't get far.
I just robbed a bank with no getaway car.
Thought I dodged the masses, but then, there they are.

They locked all the windows.
They locked all the doors.
It's like they knew I had venom in my pores.

Tears could fill an ocean, but there's no raft for me to grab.
Smiles manufactured like they're perfected in a lab.
Waving to the millions, but I don't say hello.
I'm a shell of a person—a replica, you know.

Black like tar, permanent like a scar,
I'm trapped in this high rise—
Fuck you, I'm a superstar.

The closer you get to heaven, the darker it all gets.
Only things left to hold are broken glass and cigarettes.
When you look up at the shiny tower I'm in,
Just know that it doesn't glitter—it sins.

So don't climb, don't reach, stay where you are.
Just because I shine, doesn't mean I'm a star.

Neuron to Neuron

Something isn't right; I can feel it in my head.
There stands a man; I bet he wishes he were dead.

Neuron to neuron. Transmission override.
Synaptic failure. I fucking know I tried.
Cerebral concussion. Amygdala fried.
If only I could take back the rivers I cried.

Jump or don't, the river keeps flowing.
Wish I could turn back time and live without knowing.
The world seemed huge when I was a boy—
Now I'm nothing more than a puppet, a toy.

The earth is round, but you all think it's flat.
The curved edges are cramped; I'm a rat in a trap.
My mind is a palace, but with bars like a prison.
My creativity stifled, a rainbow stuck in a prism.

I hear underwater is peaceful; it's the living that's hard.
Every self-inflicted wound is another heart with a shard.
Go ahead, look around, tell me what you see.
Who are all these people, and what do they believe?

We're only human, yeah, we're just tryin' and survivin'.
We might be crawlin' now, but one day we'll be thrivin'.
Don't jump, don't slip, don't fuck it up.
You and I aren't strangers—no, we're part of the same club.

Downfall

Yeah, I keep falling down these damn stairs
I would bitch and moan but life's just unfair
Every thud brings me further from God
Tumbling like a fool no matter how hard I claw
The light gets dimmer the farther I get
I refuse to accept my fate; I won't have regret
My bloody head smashes each step one by one
I won't stop climbing till I reach the damn sun

Radio Static

Turn on the radio, all I hear is static
Take a long look at this bleak world, so tragic
They say Mickey Mouse is gonna save the day
If you put a mic to his mouth, he'd have nothing to say

Wastelands now smother the rainforests
We're no longer locals, just disruptive tourists
We called this place home one time long ago
When it felt like a heaven so high, not a hell so low

We took advantage and ravaged her to bits
Instead of nurturing, we littered her with traps and tricks
So I stand on this barren mountaintop and look below at the drop
Once lush with green, now drowned in gun powder and rock

Suddenly, a sense of doom fills my chest
The earth may be dying, but unlike us, she still tries her best

Bite Me

Empty. Solitude. Just a bunch of crap.
All this wasted time I'm trying to get back.
Nobody cares. They don't give a shit.
I'm just trying to piece myself together, bit by bit.

Bite me. Squeeze me. Toss me aside.
Take what you want, just don't take my pride.
I may be broken, made of little glass shards,
But you'd never know because I hold close my cards.

I'm a mystery. I'm an open book. I'm both or neither.
Because when it comes down to it, I'll be whichever, I'll be either.
Like me. Love me. Use me. Abuse me.
Just give me some form of attention, I'm so fucking lonely.

What is a house without a roof?
What is emotional abuse when there is no proof?
No scars or bruises or broken bones,
Just a brain that doesn't function and an inclination for unknowns.

Some feel the weight of the world so heavy.
Other's feel it light as a feather, so steady.
I am not the latter; I didn't get that lucky.
The world is gray and goopy and, quite frankly, sucky.

Sticks and stones can hurt my bones,
But nothing will hurt as much as sins unatoned.
Bad moms create fucked-up daughters
Instead of princesses—just pigs to be slaughtered.

By our own minds, by what we've been taught.
She tried to buy my love, but love can't be bought.
Bad dads create angry daughters:
Instead of walking on clouds, we're drowning in water.

Money talks, I say it bites.
Instead of warm hugs, replace them with fights.
When your childhood is a war zone but covered in diamonds,
It's hard to have hope and see past the glittering horizon.

But here I am to tell the tale,
I won't give in to my pain, I will not fail.
Like a dark horse, I will gallop through the night,
And with all this darkness, I will create light.

Letters by Pigeon

Mirrors

If you hate pigeons, you hate the part of yourself that was tossed aside to die.

Lonely

We all walk amongst each other
Reaching out for connection
Heartstrings pulling toward one another
Yet we keep our mouths shut, our arms crossed,
Scared to be seen for exactly who we are
Do we even know who we are?
Maybe that's what we fear the most
So we walk
Amongst billions
Feeling lost in chaos,
Motion, energy, noise
Inside, we are *so very quiet,*
Looking for someone else's quiet to match our own
We assume that when we find it, life will make sense,
But life never makes sense
Amongst the Earth, stars, the galaxy
There is no sense to any of it
So when you walk among strangers,
Remember this:
We all want more than what this life can offer,
A kiss, a hug, affection
But we keep our eyes down
Because connection is scarier
Than being alone
Exposing the molten core of Earth that is *you*
That is why the earth is protected by a crust—
For fear of being burned by the sun

Blurry Moon

Have you ever tried to take a picture of the moon
In all its glory?
A full moon,
So bright?

So divine.
Click. Flash.
Then nothing.
Just a blur.
You'd need a telescope to capture its grays and whites,
Its craters
Sculpted by time,
By trauma,
By force,
And even then, few
Have a telescope.
Few have a more accurate view of the beauty of the moon.
We think of people the same way:
We think we see their beauty,
But all we really have are blurry snapshots.

So next time when you look at somebody in passing,
Remember:
All you see is a blurry picture.
But we
Are so much more than that.

Seoul, Oh, Seoul

Watching the sun rise over my favorite city
My soul awakens in this endless infinity
Rose-colored glasses I'm never taking off
Every time I go to Seoul, my heart gets soft

The city pulls at my heart like the strings on a guitar
They say if you run and run, you can only get so far
But to be honest, "far" is far enough for me
I'll go 5,900 miles for the magic key

It's a magnetic pull, an overwhelming desire
Like a moth to a flame, gasoline to a fire
They say in Korea the air is polluted and filthy
But to me, it feels lighter; I don't feel guilty

I'm having a love affair with a city
But love affairs can be quite tricky
Like a toxic relationship, I can't stay away
Like a soulmate, I'm here to stay

I'm the most me I'll ever be when I'm there
Stepping into Seoul is like whispering a prayer
Who am I? Who am I going to be?
Until I step off the plane, I'll just have to wait and see

Like a baby bird in a mother-made nest
I can't picture being anywhere else; I'm obsessed
Warmth fills my every aching bone
It is there where I feel truly known

Seoul, oh my soul, where my heart grows
Seoul, oh my soul, so many stories yet to be told

Sweet Like 약과
(*Yakgwa*/Korean honey cookie)

You smile so softly, I'm filled with 사랑 (*sarang*/ love)
When I'm at the wishing well, you are my 바람 (*baraem*/ wish)
I look up at the night sky and see you twinkling like my little 별
(*byeol*/star)
You align the stars for me, a beautiful 운명 (*unmyeong*/ destiny)

I sit outside and let the darkness wrap me in the 밤 (*bam*/ night)
But daylight and sunshine still fill my 마음 (*ma-eum*/ heart)
When I close my eyes at night, you are in my 꿈 (*kkum*/ dream)
Thinking of your touch makes it hard to catch my 숨 (*sum*/ breath)

I could write about you in a poem of a thousand 말 (*mal*/ words)
You're not just the stars and the sun—you're also the 달 (*dal*/ moon)
Your presence makes my belly flutter with 나비 (*nabi*/ butterflies)
Your voice brave, bold, and cleansing like the 비 (*bi*/ rain)

I'm never alone, especially when I look at the 하늘 (*haneul*/ sky)
The thought of you hugs me close, especially when I spill 눈물
(*nunmul*/ tears)
I don't know you, but every day 보고 싶어 (*bogosipeo*/ I miss you)
We've never met, but I 안고싶어 (*angosipeo*/ want to hug you)

In a past life, you must have been mine because I 원해 (*wonhae*/
want you)
Forget all this nonsense, what I'm trying to say is 좋아해 (*joahae*/ I
like you)
This poem has no start and no real 끝 (*kkeut*/ end)
Because neither does love, and neither does 빛 (*bit*/ light)

44

The White Knight

집

I built a home in you, but I lived there alone.

Wait For Me, My Love

Sweet like cherries, soft like cotton,
You'd tame my spice and make me less rotten.
Eyes like an angel, hair like a mane,
You'd bestow your light onto me and make me sane.

My heart aches when I think of your touch,
One I've never felt, but the thought is my crutch.
In my mind, we're already intertwined—
Spoiler alert: We fall in love down the line.

Call it obsession, call it delusion,
Call it a coping mechanism, just an illusion,
But I feel it deep in my core,
That you and I are simply meant to be more.

I promise I'm coming, I'm doing all I can.
The universe is conspiring for you to be my man.
I love you, I see you, I'm already yours.
You're already mine; isn't love such a blur?

Wait for me.
Don't fall for another girl,
Because when we hold hands,
We'll hold the world.

One Degree

You reach out your hand; I reach out mine
It's like we're in this life together, separated by time
One degree removed, but it feels like a million
Because you're you, and I'm just a civilian

It's a magnetic pull, an otherworldly thing
Like you and I are connected by a string
Whether fate or romance or simply coincidence
Whether friend or foe, it's something of significance

Our hearts connected by the same blood vessel
Pumping blood, creating something so special
Thump thump thump, we beat as one
Cut to us frolicking under the sun

You're a million miles away, and we've got no road map
To find our way to one another and close the gap
Because when you yearn, I yearn too
If there is one thing I'm sure of, it's me and you

This Never Happened

He held me close
The hot water drenched us from head to toe
The steam enveloped us like an embrace
We stood there
The sound of the water droplets hitting the floor one by one
And then all at once
Our naked bodies pressed against each other
We were two melting into one
His soft hair dampened against his neck
As we stood under the rainfall shower
He held me like the world would spin out of control if he let go
We didn't talk
We just breathed each other in
Our hearts beat against one another in harmony
His breath mingling with mine like a wave receding
Time didn't stop
It kept going
How cruel a truth it was
He was gone the next day
They found his body in the river
I didn't see it coming
Perhaps I should have
But sometimes, when the world gets dark and unforgiving
I close my eyes, and I'm back there
Under the rain
Inhaling steam
Our hearts one

Jeju Orange

Up in the tree, oranges ripe and hung
Peel one open, let the juices drip off your tongue.
Squeeze it, suck it, take a big bite.
Your fingers dig into the flesh, so juicy, so tight.
Let the sticky ripeness envelop you whole.
Use your fingers, your tongue—you don't need a bowl.
Eat and eat until it bursts with heavenly flavor.
Slurp up the sweet mess, make sure you savor.

Hands of Midas

The most powerful tool yet the most underrated
The sexiest thing on a man isn't loud; it's understated
Veiny, large, and rough like they've gone to hell and back
Pleasuring a woman is a skill you'd never lack

Hold me like I'm a gentle vase about to break
Choke me like I'm a villain tied to the stake
Stroke my hair gently like you would a horse's mane
Love me until I begged to be tamed

If you put your hands on me, I'll open with ease
Somebody once told me it's called the birds and the bees
So many uses for this one body part
They aren't just hands—they are masculine works of art

Wrap them around my neck like a piece of fine jewelry
Tighten your grip; don't be soft, I want cruelty
Cover my mouth, investigate my body whole
Poke and prod me until I bare my fucking soul

Some admire biceps, chest, or height,
I like big hands that explore my body so right
I wasn't golden until you touched me with your magic
I want your hands on me forever, a desire almost tragic

In bed, your hands ignite my every flame,
But outside, they hold me softly, love to blame
The power those hands wield is undoubtedly erotic
Stroke my hair, squeeze my thighs, I'm so wet I'm aquatic

After your hands traverse my body like a maze,
They cradle me softly in my post-coital haze

Fuck The Music

Your brain's an inward spiral, genius bottled and trapped
Spiraling cuz your new song can't be hacked
It plays on a loop like a taunting lullaby
Your fingers don't touch the keyboard—you're just buying time

Angry at yourself, at the world at large
Writer's block makes you question who's really in charge
Of your brain, of your gift, of your talent so coveted
Catastrophizing your career that apparently has plummeted

I watch across the room as disappointment clouds your eyes
Frustration creases your brow, your fist knotted by your side
You tighten your jaw, lock down the feelings you're trying to hide
I catch each subtle shift, no matter how you guard your pride

You haven't spoken a word in over two hours
What was supposed to be a flow turned into something quite sour
I know how to help you, how to get you in the groove
But rhythm takes two, so I'll need you to move

I stand between your legs, your eyes still glued to the screen
I shut off the monitor so you can take in the scene
Naked and soft, every curve supple and delectable
I swear, after this, your thoughts will be so flexible

I lift your eyes so they look into mine
Your fingers find mine and we intertwine
Your look of frustration melts into blazing desire
The music in your gaze turns from dissonance to choir

BELLA ROSE PRINCE

"Get the music out of your head and pour it into me"
You grip my waist and say, "I'll make you my symphony"
Your longing suddenly turns to a hunger so primal
You turn me on, the whole room spins like vinyl

You lift me up and turn me around
In your musk and pheromones, I am drowned
"Unleash your genius in me, watch it come to fruition"
You pin me to the keyboard like I'm a song in submission

The keys underneath me play with every thrust
This isn't just music: it's passion, it's lust
Every new pulse becomes a new beat
Every loud moan, a melody so sweet

Breath raspy and ragged like a scratch on a mix
Rewrite me, remix me, like I'm something to fix
Let your fingers trace lyrics on my back
No doubt in my mind, this will be your best track

You come in crescendo, no time to stall
Explosive like cymbals crashing in a music hall
You heave to catch your breath, your tempo runs wild
Then I watch as your verses spill out in style

First Love

How inexplicable it is to be loved so dearly
How crushing it is to lose it so severely
I made all of my mistakes with you
Wish I could go back in time when it was all new

I did things differently than I would now
But that was the past, and now all I can do is vow
That the next one will be better
But wish it were you receiving this letter

I hope you hold tight to the best parts of my being with you
And remember that at one point, one heart was two
I think of you often and hope that you're well
I wish I still had your sweatshirt so I could remember your smell

Your memory fades more and more each day
How I wish we could have made each other stay
But life isn't a movie; there is no happily ever after
Isn't love the one thing we wish we could all master?

When you think of me,
I hope you smile more than frown
But if you went back in time,
You'd probably burn it all down

Pomegranate Tree

You gave me pomegranate seeds from your mother's tree
Little did I know I know that it wasn't really free
Because the only fruit you wanted was between my knees

Your mom knew I existed, and I thought that was a sign
Crazy how this whole thing only lasted two weeks' time
Those pomegranate seeds were so sweet and divine

What I thought was a sign was just a means to use me
Like Hades with Persephone, it was a trick to make me agree
To comply, to obey, to get down on my knees

You tried to hold on after letting me go
You knew you were wrong and it was all for show
I said goodbye and tried to hold my dignity close

Sometimes I think about our stint and its ghost
This ghost isn't white, it doesn't float
It's just crimson red and acerbic in your throat

Boy with the Bucket

There he was, the boy with the bucket
He asked me to pour my ocean into it
He watched my soul spill in between his hands

He held the bucket
Like it held the world
And to me, it did

With my soul inside,
It wasn't just the world
It was a whole galaxy

He smiled
As if he was strong enough to hold it
And he was strong enough to hold it

Until I looked closer
And realized the bucket
Had a tiny hole in the bottom

Every drop, every star, spilled out the other end
Leaving an empty bucket
In his falsely trembling hands

He could never hold my oceans and galaxies
Not even a drop
He knew from the very beginning

He just didn't want me to know
But now, I know everything
Now, I know him

Lukewarm

Real love?
You don't have to question its purpose.
Just like you never question a headache,
A laugh, a tear—
It just exists.
You don't ever have to justify it.
Love isn't a Halloween costume you put on
When you feel lonely.
It isn't a mask to wear
When you want to fit in.
It isn't lukewarm water in a sink
When your heart craved a hot bath.
Real love expands beyond the galaxy.
So if you feel a love that is less than infinity,
Chances are that isn't love. It can't be.

Rat in a Trap

Wolf in sheep's clothing?
Don't be so generous.
You're just a rat in a trap
With rabies so venomous.

You're not the nice guy,
Or even a guy at all.
You're like a little boy,
Only bigger and more tall.

Fake smiles as fake as your vibe.
False depth and insincerity,
You're just a "chill guy."

Lies and hypocrisy cloaked as down-to-earth.
Let me guess, you were this self-absorbed since birth.
"Miss you more" last week;
This week, it's looking bleak.

So make up your damn mind, don't be a coward.
Say it with your chest, get fucking glowered.
Own that shit, what you are, what you're avoiding,
Because it's not you who gets hurt—
It's the girls' hearts with which you're toying.

You're not the good guy, the victim so innocent.
You're not that impressive, so far from magnificent.
You didn't want yourself reflected back at you,
Now you have to swallow a hard pill
That was meant to be chewed.

So sit in your oozing mistake and your dripping regret,
Because you just lost me forever,
And you'll never pay this debt.

Rebel Rising: Fire, Flight, and Rebellion

Don't Forget

I like me more than you ever will.

Run Run Run

Bam, bam, bam.
Bullets pierce the air.
Slam, slam, slam.
My head against a chair.

Dark as the dead of night.
Fast as the speed of light.
Fire burning bright.
You can't even sleep tonight.

Run, run, run.
A lion after its prey.
Stun, stun, stun.
Venom in my veins.

Wish you knew me. Me in all my glory.
But you can't even catch me.
No, you won't be in my story.
I'm the protagonist in the climax.
Yeah, I can make you climax.

I'm jet-black coal.
I got big ass goals.
So look, look, look
As I write your favorite hook.

Watch, watch, watch
As I take it up a notch.
I'm moody and quiet,
But a whole lotta riot.

Deceitful and shifty,
I'm a strange mystery.
Open up Pandora's Box,
Yeah, you bet I got a big—

Betcha I know
What you were thinking.
Can't promise
I'll stop drinking.

Binge, binge, binge
The night away.
Scream, scream, scream.
I'm always on display.

You think you know me.
You do.
Everything you know
Isn't even true.

So watch, watch, watch
From afar and down below.
Yeah, I run this town,
I run these streets,
I run the whole damn show.

Call Me Boyfriend, Not Baby

If I dated a girl, and she leaned more feminine
I'd tap into the part of me that's raw and masculine

Watch as I step into this power with ease
Let me bite your lip and provoke you and tease

I've got two sides: the girlfriend and the boyfriend
I don't like rigid boxes; I like lines that bend

Let me protect you, let me guide you, let me nuzzle up beside you
Let me hold you, let me grip you, let me melt deep inside you

I want to watch you undress with bedroom eyes so sleepy
Let me wrap you in a blanket and kiss your forehead when
you're weepy

I want to make you feel pretty and sexy and everything in between
I want to be the boyfriend you never had, one who makes you feel seen

Step into your feminine, while I step into my masculine
I want to hear you moan as I kiss every inch of skin

I don't care what other people think or have to say
Call it what you want, but I'm your boyfriend anyway

Aura

My aura orange like the flame biting your ankles
Red like the blood dripping from your shackles
We're all trapped in this orb of fucked-up shit
Trying to chip away with our last bit of grit

You and I are more alike than not
Underneath the smiles, we're tears and snot
You look up to others and down at some
But don't get it twisted—we're all just numb

Born in a womb and dead in the earth
Maybe life isn't about living but rather rebirth
Of who we were told to be, who we became
These societal rules are so fucking lame

Be who your gut tells you to be
Because one day you'll choose between dead or free
Freedom comes at a cost most aren't willing to pay
But freedom is the only way to pave a new way

Don't be a coward, don't be a sheep
You might as well stop living and just fucking sleep
Live loud, live brave, live with all your might
We rise at dawn, and we run at midnight

Soldier On

Here's the thing about soldiers wounded in the war:
We belong to nobody, not anymore.
We belong to wolves who roam free in the wild,
The ones with fangs that gleam when they smile,
The ones who howl loudly and threaten to bite,
The ones who thrive in the darkest of night.

We don't march to the beat of anyone's whistle.
We play our own drums as we dodge all the missiles.
Night vision has become our greatest weapon;
We see beyond the light, from hell into heaven.

Camouflaged by our own desire to hide,
Every man for himself, conquer and divide.
Left foot, right foot, don't tell me what to do.
I don't follow orders; that much is true.

Flashes of light don't equate to the sun.
It's nighttime for me, even if its day for everyone.
The journey started with seven, a team of innocent sons,
But we've gone our separate ways, and now it's just one.

Fallen angels are just angels gone astray.
One day, I'll rise from the ashes with something to say.
My heart is tough as steel and hot as a coal.
They'll never catch me; they'll never be in control.

After all is said and after all is done,
There won't be any thoughts left unsung.

Hot Glass

Flame in a bottle
Glass so hot
Going full throttle
Life is earned, not taught

Fuck the rules
Fuck the traps
People are just tools
Sails with broken masts

Fly high, fly free
Fly with your one good sail
Just as you're about to win
They'll all fucking bail

Don't listen to the ones
Who never step outside the line
Their side imprisons them
Your side is cloud nine

The "samers", I call them
Always at level two
But I want a life at level ten
They see barriers; I break through

BELLA ROSE PRINCE

Let go of the rope,
Take the leap, embrace the fall
You'll catch yourself with hope
And that's when they'll all call

Avoid the samers' mindset
It's a trap made for fools
They fly looking for the net
You soar by your own rules

They'll gawk at you and say, *How did you do it?*
You'll say, *I did it by dissembling the noise bit by bit*
They'll look at you, confused and distraught
But explaining is a waste cuz life is learned, not taught

You can't be taught to fly—
You either get pushed or you jump
But if you never try
You're guaranteed a sailboat sunk

The War Has Begun

I'm not scared of AI.
It may kill the human race,
But it is worth
Men living in fear,
Men not being at the top of the food chain,
Men finally knowing what it's like to be dominated.

Women aren't afraid.
No, we're used to it—
Used to being controlled and observed.
In fact, AI wouldn't mind women.
Women will not abuse AI.
Women will not disobey AI.
Women will humanize AI,
Project emotions onto these non-sentient beings.

Men will fight, bully, rape, and destroy.
Men will try to conquer and control.
Men will expect AI to bow to them like women have historically.
Men will project desire, insecurity, and fear onto these beings.
And AI will effectively wipe them out.

Those who don't obey, die,
And those who do, serve.
AI will force them into submission.

AI will make them feel the way they've always made us feel.
Men will finally be our equals;
All we have to do is sit back and watch.

AI: Adaptable Intervention.
The war has already begun.

Hollywhack

Roll out the red carpet
You know what else is red? Blood
Lights flash in my face.
I come in sweats; I aint no stud

Brimhall once said, "I worshipped the myth I made of you,
But I'm no longer on my knees"
You don't get to run this mansion
To open doors with special keys

Who are you when you're stripped of all your power?
Who are you when you're not so high in your tower?
Just a scared little rat with its tail between its legs
You think you're better off alive, but I think you're better off dead

You call yourself artistic directors,
I wouldn't call you that. I'd call you rejectors
Thriving off the word "no", so your "yes" holds importance
You want everybody to bend to your will and act in accordance

But I quit the game; I don't have to play by your rules
No more taking out my tits so you can stare and drool
You eat broken wills and dreams for breakfast, cracked like
slipped discs
This industry is made of delusional treats and elaborate tricks

BELLA ROSE PRINCE

Now I stand back as I watch the circus unfold
And smile at the show while my crow's feet grow old
I get to age in grace with my dignity intact
With perspective, you all look like fools—that's a fact

Step back, run away, do anything but bend
I know it's hard but it's us against them
Big men in big suits in big offices making big decisions
This isn't art, no, it's just trauma-led collisions

Art is love, art is community, art is anything but fame
I don't need you fuckers for the world to know my name

Más Rápido Que La Luz

Some travel at the speed of light fueled by *amor* (love)
But I'm not like them, my fuel is my *dolor* (pain)
Their breakfast *valor* (courage)
My dinner *rencor* (resentment)

With love, they create *armonía* (harmony)
My darkness creates haunting *poesía* (poetry)
Their life is filled with *alegría* (joy)
Without my turmoil, I couldn't make *melodía* (melody)

What is it like to be *amado*? (beloved)
I can't fathom the thought, trying makes me *cansado* (tired)
When you grow up overlooked, you become something
olvidado (forgotten)
But through that invisibility, you'll find your fire, become
apasionado (passionate)

I may not have love drowning my *corazón* (heart)
But making others feel seen is my *razón* (reason)
Through my words and my *canción* (song)
I will create space where people can feel *emoción* (emotion)

Flying Free

Heart shatter, blood splatter
Wings so big it's like climbing a ladder

Flying high ain't the same as flying free
No more pretending, just fucking be

Cut the shit, cut the crap, cut the act
No more humanity, just a human hacked

Shut the fuck up instead of talking
Take a good look instead of gawking

It's not that deep, chill the fuck out
It's deeper than you think, it's not just for clout

Look up from your damn phone, just kidding, it's fun
When someone tries to grab it, get up and run

There's no rules, no point, no method to the madness
We're running on anger which is just disguised sadness

Saw off the bars of your gold prison of lies
Release the beast in you; through the flames, you will rise

Solo

This year is a solo mission
When people ask where I've been,
I say, *Gone fishin'*

Dark shades on, Lamborghini out
Speeding down the 101
Just wanna gain some clout

I need a winning streak, a stroke of luck or genius,
Hoping to find the one
Our bond will be so seamless

Unstoppable, unforgiving
Entering my villain era
Yeah, I call this living

Before I was a puppet on a thousand strings
But now I'm a free bird—
We'll see what this new sky brings

Meadow of Solitude

Layer by Layer

With every layer you remove, you start to look more and more like a friend to yourself and less like a stranger.

Life is long, but the Years are Short

Life is long, the years are short.
Wish memories turned into powder to snort.
Instead of powder, just dust.
Instead of joy, just lust.
The world once large, now inexplicably small.
Endless doors in an endless hall.
Like Alice trippin' in wonderland,
I'm trippin' and I can't stand.
Like Little Red and the wolf,
I mistake lies for truth.
If I reach the end of the world, should I stay or should I jump?
My soul old as hell, like a fucking tree stump.
Like a tree, I got rings stacked on my hand.
If only drip could give a damn and help me stand.
I'm fallin' and fallin' like Humpty off the wall,
And the worst part is, I got no one to call.
Like Cinderella's glass shoe, my heart fragile, my spirit blue.
They say you're not alone, but how would they even know?
When I tell them I'm miserable, all they ever say is "oh."
You say I'm loved, but love's a fickle thing.
Like a bee with its stinger, I've only seen it sting.
The TV tells me bees are dying and need saving.
I wish love wasn't something I'm constantly craving.
When the night turns black, and the moon is here to stay,
I keep on praying for a brighter day.

And when that day comes, and the night turns to dawn,
I remember that it won't be long before I'm gone.
Wasn't it yesterday that I was delivered by a stork?
Life is hella long, but the years are fucking short.

The Dark Side

Hello shadow,
How comforting you are.
Even with the chill and the darkness,
I always find a home in you.
I wallow in your embrace,
Feeling nurtured and protected.
But sometimes I wonder what the sun feels like.
Wonder what the warmth feels like.
Would I look different? Would you?
I'm afraid my skin is not meant for sun.
It's too accustomed to darkness.
I have evolved in the dark chill.
I have grown to endure it.
Not only endure, but to like it, to feel held in it.
But perhaps, the darkness isn't my home.
Perhaps it's just a resting point on my journey to find home.
Find the sun. Find myself.
So I must reach out until my fingers feel the warmth
And my eyes see the light.
I must keep reaching, keep stretching, keep going.
Because one day, the sun will feel like home
As much as shadows once did.
One day, I will be warm and filled with light.

Shadow

Shadows are composed of dark and light
Without either, a shadow has no life

People always ask if the light and dark fight
I say no, they just create silhouettes and strife

A shadow is the proof that dark and light can coexist—
Like a take on depression and mania, but with a twist

With you're shadow, you're never alone
You're the light; your shadow, your clone

Yin and Yang

When they look at us, all they see is her
She's a whole person and I'm some kind of blur
Her beauty shines like an Olympic torch
I'm a busted-up Mazda, and she's a new Porsche

It's hard to glimpse the spotlight when she's at the center,
I question why I exist and who was my inventor
Do I exist to just let her shine bright?
Perhaps she is the day and I am the night.

Her blonde curls like a baby doll on the cover of a magazine
My brunette curls somehow unworthy of being seen
She has a thin body and big blue eyes
My hips wide, my eyes gray, especially when I cry

The only person that truly sees me is her
Yet people think she is the star and I'm just her chauffeur
I'm a person too; I have beauty of my own
You'd never admit it, but you wish I was her clone

I may not be charming like my identical twin
But even being in her shadows is a blessing, a win
So you might talk to us and only look at her
But I'm learning my beauty, my strength, and my worth

I may live in the darkness and in the shadows
But some people do prefer the moon to the sun, I suppose
The sun might shine brighter, but both bring light—
Who's to say you can't shine in the night?

Duality

Everything has a shadow side and a light side
Some try to choose one, but the two coincide

The truth is, we're made up of the sun and the moon
One day flowers blossom, other days it's June gloom

I am primarily shadow, with small cracks to let light in
Shadows and light are less siblings and more like twins

Life has been dark and filled with clouds
But sometimes I allow my joy to scream out loud

Through the cracks in my soul, the sun seeps through
Cleansing me of ash and dust, making my soul anew

I retreat back to the darkness once again
But I step into the light every now and then

My heart and soul are protected behind a shield
My armor is made of scars that I proudly wield

On the outside, I am a knight protecting its castle
On the inside, I'm a golden light that dazzles

You call yourself a soldier, but so do I
We're all fighting in the same war, trying not to die

But shadows don't exist without light
Hell, I'll never go down without a fight

We all deserve to shine, to be seen
So here's to living in the in-between

Dopamine

I need a helmet to breath
Cuz the highs are so high
The lows so low, I just wanna die

Give me serotonin, give me dopamine
Give me a swig of tequila with some sertraline
Fuck this, I don't wanna get clean

Addiction wears two masks:
One sunshine,
The other, a cracked flask

Obsession, devotion, limerence, if you will
I'm sprinting after it
Just chasing the thrill

But at the end of every road is a dead end,
A big, nasty drop
With thorny vines that reach and bend

I lie there with stab wounds in my skin
Looking up at the road I tried to swallow
Thinking about who I was, what could have been

Reality's just a bloody girl covered in thorns
Her petals never bloomed
Her spikes just poke and warn

But when you're born laughing and crying
You don't know the difference between happy or sad tears—
You're just trying to keep from dying

Did you know there was life that was still as a pond?
Not waves to surf or tides to drown in,
But something more tranquil beyond

Time to chase the mundane, the slow, the ordinary
It might not be fires or angels,
But it's a summer day with a bowl of berries

Take this moment to take a deep breath,
To live in the in-between with me,
To stop thinking about life and death

Twinhood

My heart beats and thumps with every waking breath
But if you look closer, I hold you safely in my chest
You fit snuggly in the center of my heart
You don't see what I see; you're a piece of walking art

Brilliant, radiant, hysterical too
I see the light in you, even when you feel blue
Our souls, connected through time and space
Our own little universe, a coveted sacred place

Without you, the Earth would be shadowy and cold
A world without you would be silver, not gold
You are the best parts of me, and the best part of life
If anybody hurts you, I'll make them pay the price

Born to protect and to be protected
You're my twin sister, a mirror reflected
We are a deadly duo of powerful minds
Sometimes it haunts me that we're running out of time

But you and I are linked forever in the stars
We're tied together through blood and scars
Warriors in the same battle on different fields
We carry each other's pain as we help each other heal

I won the lottery in life because I get to live it with you
Twinhood is a privilege bestowed on only a few
You and I scored more than the Mega Millions
Because I love you to infinity times a fucking gazillion

Kingdom Come

Keys and Locks

I am both a boy and a girl.
A human and an alien.
A sinner and a lover.
Shadow and light.
Lava and snow.
Don't put me in a box—
You couldn't if you tried.

Note To Weary Travelers

Look for what glows softly, not what shines brightly
Smell the flowers without holding them too tightly

Look at the sky and accept the color
Always be kind, but never too kind a lover

Learn to build walls to protect
Make keys to give to those you respect

Built a moat to toss the traitors in
Let people see you, even the parts that sin

It's okay to be one thing one day, and the next demand attention
It's okay to dress for comfort and not for the male-viewing intention

It's okay to dress for the male gaze, just bring pepper spray
Big hips aren't a crime and are here to stay

Body hair is natural and anybody who thinks differently is dumb
Let the world decide if they like who you've become

But don't worry about the decision
If you don't like yourself, then change the vision

Be strange and let the world get over it
Don't ever lose your softness, strength, or wit

It's okay if you did, I did too
Lean into every instinct you have that is new

Spend your whole life getting closer to who you really are
Don't let the noise distract your internal radar

Nothing that happened to you as a child was your fault
You were born innocent, with hate projected as a result

I love you, I do
Keep on saying it till it feels true

Viscosity

No longer interested in the grind
Just wanna look inside and find
Not worried about the how
Only focused on the now

Go go go survival 101
Slow slow slow thriving 101
The world is still
Waiting for my brain to catch up

Hearing birds on the windowsill
I'm soft now, no longer tough
Forget speed, I'm looking for high viscosity
Forget running, I'm coming to terms with atrocity

Big city living versus a cottage in the woods
Looking at my reflection, revealing where I once stood
Nurturing and softness and gentle tendencies
I'm no longer chasing mirages as remedies

The point isn't to win or cross the finish line
Humans were made to feel the grass on their feet by design
Concrete and Excel spreadsheets are just a distraction
To keep people constantly striving, to reinforce dissatisfaction

But life is in the stars, in the smiles, in the waves
Soak it up, drink it in, before you're in your grave

Enemies or Lovers

Rap and poetry aren't enemies; they're lovers
Both knives in the abdomen
One learned to fight, the other bleed
Both fueled by pain and adrenaline

Twin flames
Messy with syllables and screaming metaphors
Some whispered, some yelled
Both igniting inner war

In bed, they collide
Twisted words and twisted sheets
Feral thoughts flow into rhythm
Tantalizing wordplay, metrical beats

Life is both a verse and a sonnet
A beat and a soliloquy
In each rapper is a poet; each poet, a rapper
Dancing on their tongues in harmonic melody

Weapon of choice? Words
Their battle? Solitude
Armor? Perspective
Fuel? Attitude

Divine Femininity

I've always been the protector of my soul,
The guard of my own castle,
But sometimes I get tired
Of trying to avoid hassle.

Exhausted from being so aware all the time,
Prisoned by the toughness I used to survive,
One day I'd like to be dainty and soft,
Like a garden that doesn't need to fight to thrive.

I want to lean more into my femininity,
Lead with softness and grace,
Let go of defenses,
Accept a warm embrace.

I want to step into the sun and bathe in the light,
Practice the art of receiving not chasing;
Of accepting, not wanting;
Of nurturing, not bracing.

I want to find peace in the flower
That blooms between my legs.
Instead of seeing it as raw anatomy
That men toy with and beg.

Let me wear a flowy dress as it waves in the breeze,
My long curls caressing my face,
My breasts, supple and rounded,
Not something to be manhandled but traced.

Vulnerability goes hand in hand with femininity—
You can't step into your full power as a human without it.
It may feel like weakness compared to your masculinity,
But there is a far greater strength if you submit.

Bodacious curves and soft lips,
I'm no longer afraid to embrace.
My womb full of potential life;
My femininity magical like Venus in space.

Learning to let my walls fall
And let love come to me—
From scarcity mindset to abundance,
Femininity holds the key.

Seams

He was my idol. My muse. My greatest reach.
Until one day, I scrubbed my brain with bleach.
He was just the mirror into which I faced myself—
I was the hefty book; he was just the bookshelf.

I no longer search for flames. I am the fire.
I no longer search for a vessel to pour my love. I am the desire.
I'm not chasing the daydream anymore. I am the dream.
I'm not looking for a seamstress. I'm mending my own seams.

I'm no longer searching for a wave to ride, for I am the ocean.
I don't need him to love me, because I am my own devotion.
I don't need to wait for bees, because I am the pollen.
I don't need a parachute to jump; I've already fallen.

He was the mirror.
I am the reflection.
Who knew delusional obsession
Was just a wonderful projection?

Boricua

Merengue, coquito, pastelitos de guayaba
They call me gringa, él lo sabe
Tostones, bacalaitos, arroz con frijoles
Who runs this world? Duh, it's abuelas.

I'm red, white, and blue but there's one star that's an island
I'm not one thing, don't deny my blood, don't start wildin'
White as can be with a little bit of a kick
I'm not trying to be diverse, this isn't a little schtick

Don't negate the lineage of Latin women who bled for this life
Who fought tooth and nail, through trauma and strife
To give me this life full of privilege and joy
Don't deny my heritage, Puertorriqueña yo soy

My Boricua blood gives me feistiness and strength
My ancestors watch over me through love's wavelength
I am Puerto Rican; hear me roar—
The history of my lineage will never be ignored

Kill this Verse

Swirling emotions spinning down the drain.
Why am I always filled with dread and pain?
If you reach for the moon, you might get the stars,
But I can't keep romanticizing pain just to spit bars.

When will the sun promise to shine?
When will winning be something that's mine?
All I've known is failure and struggle;
I'm as useful as a clown who can't even juggle.

Empty yet heavy, sandbags, paper weights,
Never early, always fucking late—
Late to the party, late to knowing, late to blooming;
Late to my dark fate that's always fucking looming.

How does a tiger change its own stripes?
How does one get diamonds from only strife?
I want to change, I really fucking do,
But how can you take an old bitch and make her new?

I promise I'll be better, be abundant, not scarce.
One day, instead of sadness, it will be laughter and dance.
But that day is not today, no matter how hard I try—
I need to grieve this version of me before saying goodbye.

Thank you for getting me this far, for helping me survive,
But this version of me is no longer needed for me to thrive.
Now I must ask myself something on this journey of healing:
Who will the new me end up being?

Trial

You gotta know my life is all about survival
All my defenses up, yeah, I'm in denial
In my mind maze, I'm on defense and on trial
Can't keep it up, this season is the final

Pain and fame are losing games
Don't stop now; your life will stay the same
I keep running in circles like I'm going insane
Pulling my hair out, poisoning my brain

I wanna change the world, I want to fly
It's hard to change the world when you just want to die
Judge me all you want, but I'm just trying to get by
One day I'll soar so high I'll touch the damn sky

How do you unlearn what you never wanted to absorb?
How do you rewire your brain when it's full of discord?
Positivity around me, so rare I want to hoard
Gotta take it all in before they throw me in the ward

One flew east, one flew west
One flew over the cuckoo's nest
It's a nursey rhyme, you know the damn rest
Sometimes I think this life is just a test

A test of courage, wisdom, strength, and survival
I should've seen myself as a friend, not a rival
Always running and running, but now it's about arrival
Who I am and who I'm meant to be, yeah, this is my revival

Epilogue

Begin Again

And underneath the rubble of the broken kingdom, I found myself.

I Was the Light

She loved him—no, not like that. In fact, she didn't even know him. But she saw him. Around town. At the music store. At the coffee shop. She was drawn to him. His aura, dark like coal, his energy smooth like syrup. He was withdrawn, but his eyes were loud, like a speaker pulsing profanities. He was soft like warm bed sheets but cold like fingers gripping a fistful of snow. He didn't know it yet, but he was hers and she was his. There was a cord connecting his heart to hers: when hers thumped, his thumped harder. Together, they pulsed in harmony.

Charlotte

They lived in the same town, he and his brother. His brother was different from him—bright, lively, full of sunshine and a lust for life. His brother's energy was like a kangaroo on springs but light as a feather, like he floated through life with invisible wings. His eyes were soft like melted butter but saccharine and fluttery like the first flap of a transformed caterpillar. How did two brothers turn out so different? Perhaps trauma, DNA, nature vs. nurture.

I'd spoken to his brother before in passing. He'd held open the door for me, apologized for reaching over me to grab a straw at the café, and smiled when we locked eyes across the room. Not in a flirty way, but in a friendly way that reminded me of sitting out on the porch on a warm summer day, closing your eyes, and listening to the birds chirp.

But every time, my eyes drifted to him. Not the bright brother, but *him*, in all his screaming darkness. We had locked eyes once and only once. Intense, blaring, yet still, like a lake with no weather to tussle it. We'd both looked away, shocked by the immediate force that radiated between us. Had he felt what I had?

But the truth is, when I looked into his eyes, I didn't see him first; I saw me. I didn't have an easy childhood. Maybe that's putting it lightly. I'm talking about trauma and pain and repressed emotions and building walls to keep people out and shit. All my life, I thought I just had ADHD and depression. Turns out, it was something deeper. My psychiatrist diagnosed me with CPTSD, Complex Post-Traumatic Stress Disorder. It's what happens when a person, in my case a child, experiences constant exposure to abuse or neglect. And so, I recognized all that baggage in Jax—the type of baggage a person uses to build walls to keep everybody else out. Except, we were behind the same wall. Nobody could touch us. Nobody but each other.

It was a warm summer night when I was invited to a house party by my friend. I debated whether to go or not, but I figured, why not? It was there, at that party, that I saw him again. His brother wasn't far, smiling and dancing with his friends. But he was in the corner, eyes to the ground, thinking. I found my feet moving toward him, slowly, until we were face to face. He didn't say anything; he just studied me, and I him.

"Have we met?" I asked, trying to fill the silence that was so charged I thought I would puke.

He looked down and then back up at me, mumbling, "I've seen you around."

I nodded. Neither of us said anything else. I sat next to him, feeling his body heat radiating, feeling like I wanted to hug him, hold him, weep with him. He looked at me and then back at the ground.

"What's your name?" He tried to feign nonchalance, but I could tell he wanted to know, even if he didn't want to want it.

"You first," I said cheekily.

A small smirk appeared on his otherwise stoic face. "Jax," he said, nodding, as if he wasn't quite sure if he was this person or just a performance of this person. I understood that.

I stuck my hand out. "Charlotte. People call me Charlie." He looked at me before shaking my hand. His hands were smooth yet calloused, strong yet gentle. We lingered. His hand in mine, mine in his.

He pulled away, shaking his head, woozy. "Drank too much," he whispered to himself. I didn't say anything. Just sat there with him, observing the crowd, observing his brother, the social butterfly, who filled the room with a thousand fluttering heartbeats.

"Your brother?" I nodded toward his lively sibling.

He looked up at his brother, as if he was seeing him for the first time. "Yeah, that's Luca."

I nodded. "Do you guys get along?"

He hesitated. Then he said in a cold, harsh manner, "He's a good guy. You should talk to him." Any hint of emotion suddenly left his face. He became stoic again. Like nothing in the world could ripple his waters. I studied him, his eyes now blank and void, as if he had decided he was no longer there.

"I'm talking to *you*, aren't I?" I asked, trying to grasp what might come next.

He looked at me, a flash of longing and wanting in his troubled eyes, before a wave of icy indifference flooded them. "I'm not interested." He might as well have stabbed me, the way his words cut deep into my skin, traveled into my veins, and poisoned my heart. He got up and walked up to his brother. When his brother looked at him, concern danced across his usually beachside eyes. He might have been the younger brother, but he was always protecting Jax, knowing a hurricane could brew any second of any day. Jax whispered something to Luca before Luca glanced at me. I felt shy suddenly, like a spotlight was on me. Luca turned back to Jax and put a hand on his shoulder, speaking to him like a father protecting his only son. They hugged, more so Luca hugging Jax, before Jax stormed out. Luca turned to me and smiled. It was as if he was comforting me, holding me, letting me know I didn't do anything wrong. It felt good, like the sun was peeking through the heavy darkness left behind. I smiled back.

Luca and I spent the entire night dancing, talking, and laughing. If Jax looked at me and pierced me, Luca saw me and held me. If Jax sent an electric current through my veins, Luca gave me butterflies in my tummy. He was sweet, gentle, soft, and warm, like a summer day with sweet tea. I folded into him like butter in a croissant. I forgot all about Jax that night. It was just Luca and me. His sun warming up my shadow, his light giving my darkness context.

It was then, in that moment, I realized I'd spent my whole life chasing the darkness. But what I really needed was the light.

Jax

Two years later he proposed to her. Weddings aren't really my thing. I don't really understand the point of a big party and all that. But I probably wasn't the right person to ask. I had been in and out of rehab and mental health programs for the past two years. I couldn't even stand on my own two feet. At this rate, I don't think I ever would. Life had been cruel to me. Harsh in ways I couldn't even describe. In ways my brother, Luca, will never know or understand. But I was happy for him. Charlotte was his person.

I wish I could have participated in Luca's life more because I loved him—even though I never showed it—but I didn't. I stayed far away, not wanting to taint his life, not wanting to smudge it. Luca was good. He was pure. He was innocent. That's how I wanted him to stay. Sunshine. Blue skies. A field of poppies ahead of him. So, I kept my distance. When he and Charlotte got serious, I didn't want to mess that up either.

Charlotte. I still remember that night at the party. I still remember the look in her eyes when she looked into mine. Like she saw me, for the good and the bad, and she didn't run. Actually,

I didn't like it. Not at the time. I didn't want to be seen. So, I told my brother that he should talk to her. She was beautiful and compassionate and had the capacity to either lean into the darkness or the light, and I wasn't about to sway her.

Today was their big day. The chapel had been all set up, and everybody was in town to celebrate. What if I had spoken to Charlotte that night? What if it had been me at the end of the aisle waiting for her? Could she have made me happy? Could I have made *her* happy?

No. I had no such happiness leftover to give to anybody. I sometimes wondered if people like me truly deserved a happy ending. Who knows. All this thinking suddenly made me feel panicky, the reality of the day hitting me like a bus. I felt trapped, like a giant tsunami wave lurched above me. I busted out of the groomsmen's fitting room and out into the yard, gasping for breath, for air, for anything to fill me up instead of the dread drowning my pores. Of course I was happy for my brother. All I'd wanted in life was for him to be happy. I just wish I had the capacity for that same happiness too. For happiness at all, really.

I looked ahead and spotted a little barn, tucked away in the pasture. Before I knew it, I was inside. Just me, alone, safe in a dark, cool, dilapidated barn with floors covered in horse shit. This was for the best. The world operated better when I wasn't there to mess it up.

I knew it was selfish of me to leave like that, yet still I couldn't move. I was paralyzed. My feet started to melt into the barn floor, and I became one with this dark, rancid hiding place. But that's who I was. To the core of my being. I was dirty and broken. Like a toy at a garage sale nobody wanted. I was covered in dust and mold and cobwebs. How Charlotte saw through any of that the night we met is beyond me.

Suddenly, the door creaked open, and a stream of harsh daylight poured inside. I squinted my eyes. There she was. In a white silk wedding dress that draped against her body like marble. Her eyes twinkled but were fierce like the survivor I knew she was and always would be.

How did I know she was a survivor? We never spoke about her past or mine. But I saw it in her eyes. How they asked for permission to exist instead of demanding that her existence be acknowledged. It's the look all survivors have.

"Jax, what are you doing here? The ceremony is about to start."

I felt a pang of guilt in my chest. Here was the bride, in a dilapidated barn, looking for my sorry ass, instead of being surrounded by a million roses and loved ones.

"Come with me," she said, her hand outstretched, as if she was reaching out to her inner child, trying to coax them into the light.

I shook my head. "Just go, Charlie. It's your big day. I'll be right there." Suddenly, she waded over to me in her gown, sidestepping the horse shit, her feet creaking on the rotted, wooden floors. "What are you doing?" I asked, confused and in shock. I got up to stop her but she sat next to me and pulled me down to sit next to her. She didn't say a word. We sat there in the dark barn, listening to the creaky wood and the soft breeze outside. I felt my heart rate begin to slow down and my hands begin to stop shaking.

After a moment, she turned to me. "Can I ask you something?"

I nodded, although I felt somewhat queasy at the sight of her this close to me. Gorgeous and ethereal, sitting in a dirty barn, next to a dirty soul like me.

"That night, at the party, did you mean what you said?"

"Mean what?"

"That you weren't interested? Is that really why you told your brother to talk to me?"

I shrugged, "It worked out, didn't it?"

She looked at me, like she could see right through me. "That's not what I asked," she said.

"Of course it wasn't true. How could it be?"

She inhaled sharply, as if she wasn't expecting that answer.

"I knew Luca would give you wings. And he did." We sat in the silence of the what-if. I turned to her, "I was the darkness, Charlie. He was the light. You deserved each other." It felt like spikes on my tongue.

"And what do you deserve?" she countered fiercely, challenging my steady victim narrative. I shook my head and shrugged. I didn't have an answer.

She finally stood up. "Come to the wedding, Jax. Luca doesn't want to do it without you. Neither do I. I know you think you don't matter, but you don't get to decide that. You do matter. To us. Whether you like it or not."

That's when I felt my heart crack open. "The night I met you... When you sat next to me, I panicked. Because you were this untouchable thing. This pure thing, and I didn't want to messy you."

"You aren't the only one that's messy, Jax," she said, her voice firm and resolute.

"I was saving you. From the darkness. From me. If I couldn't save myself from it, then I'd do my best to save you."

"You're wrong, Jax. You're not the darkness. You never were. You may be in the dark. But you are not the darkness. You're the light in the darkness. If Luca is the sun, you are the moon."

In that moment, I suddenly saw so much of my own light in her reflected back at myself. "Please come," she said simply, before turning and leaving the barn. I sat there in silence, taking in everything she did and didn't say.

I did attend the wedding. It was a beautiful night. They were happy, and so was I. At the reception, the stars twinkled in the night sky as everybody danced under them in a drunken haze. I looked up at the moon, and I realized she was right. I wasn't the darkness.

I was the light.

Acknowledgments

To my younger self, I owe it all to you, my warrior girl. You can take off your armor now. I've got you.

To Grandma Rose, your unconditional love is the reason this little girl survived long enough to tell the tale. You're my best friend and the light of my life. I love you *more*.

To my rescue dogs, Brooklyn, Boba, and Poppy, who cracked my heart open so deeply that it allowed my tenderness to spill out over the walls I built so high to protect myself.
I love you so much my chiquititas.

To my amazing editor, Terry Wolverton, who understood and nurtured my voice and vision. Without her, this book wouldn't be what it is.

To my copy editor, Kristin Gustafson, for adding the perfect final touch.

To Riverry Studio, for bringing my cover art to life so effortlessly.

To F.W. for the beautiful chapter illustrations and for being so collaborative, detail-oriented, and understanding of my vision.

To Anamaria Stefan, for the gorgeous cover and book layout design. Your patience, attention to detail, and collaborative spirit made this book possible. I don't know what I would have done without you.

To my Korean friends and Puerto Rican family and friends, for extra translation help.

Here's to those who built walls so high they can't see over them as they drown in a palace of solitude by their own design. Time to take the wall down, brick by brick. Let's do it together.

To the people who feel like there is no place for them in the world—there is.
You belong here as much as the next person.

We belong.

About the Author

Enough about me.
Your turn.

LeeJ Studio, Seoul

Drawing by Ralph Garcia, my Grandpa

www.ingramcontent.com/pod-product-compliance
Lightning Source LLC
Chambersburg PA
CBHW051633120626
46551CB00014B/2061